HIJA DE TU MADRE

Poems by

Nancy Frenesy Azcona

ATREVIDA

Hija De Tu Madre // ATREVIDA

ISBN: 979-8-9915566-1-3

Cover art by Elizabeth Moroni

Edited by K.C. Cullinan and Oisín Rowe

www.gameoverbooks.com

The truth is, if we don't write our own stories, there is someone else waiting to do it for us. And those people, waiting with their pens, often don't look like we do and don't have our best interests in mind.

Hanif Abdurraqib, *They Can't Kill Us Until They Kill Us*

With your big heart, you praise God above, but how's it working out for you, honey? Do you feel loved?

Florence + The Machine, *Patricia*

Table of Contents

Prologue

Hija De Tu Madre is a Spanish slang term that means damn you, but my mother would say it to me in more of an exclamation or an "oh my god" kinda way. For example, *gasp "Hija de tu madre, no tiene vergüenza?!"* when I would leave the house without a bra or when I was younger and didn't like showering (by the way, why do kids hate showering so much???). The direct translation is "Daughter of your Mother". I've been told countless times that my mom and I are a lot alike, specifically by my brother, specifically when she and I fight. Hard-headed, fiery warriors that do everything out of love, even when we don't see that we are squeezing on too tightly.

I left New York eight years ago, but every time I come back home I am greeted with roses and freshly cut fruit. New sheets on the bed and the fan or heater already set up because she knows I always run too hot or too cold. It's a tenderness, a sweet type of love that at times is forgotten when phone calls end abruptly or in tears. The arguments happen less often now, but when they do I think it's because we both are holding on to fairytale dreams. She, wishing I was a God-fearing, married doctor with probably two children by now. And I, wishing she just *saw* me.

Atrevida means ballsy in Spanish. Another common saying my mother gently crowns me with. I always laugh when she side-eyes me when I tell her about my adventures. When I stay out a little too late in Brooklyn, or when I go on solo trips to foreign countries, or simply take a hike alone. *Atrevida.* The woman who crossed borders, the first of nine. She came here with no money and no familiar faces. She tells me the stories of her survival. Found her way from LA to Oakland, to Reno, to eventually Brooklyn. Single mother that managed to keep the lights on for two children. Studied with me night and day for her citizenship. Became a property owner. Made her own business from her love of cooking. Defied all odds. *Atrevida.* As I said, my mother and I are much alike.

My mother found Christianity later in her life and for years, she and I attended services together several times a week. I know she holds on to this hope that I will return to the path of the dutiful servant I once was. She desperately wants me to write about God. And I have, in so many ways.

This book is riddled with stories of our relationship and our once-shared religion. Stories of my identity. Stories of hurt from my own past, for my communities. Stories of love and joy triumphing in the most unlikely of situations. Every part of my life is coated with her essence, whether directly or indirectly.

Prólogo

Hija De Tu Madre es un término de la jerga española para decir maldito seas, pero mi madre me lo diría más como una exclamación o una especie de "oh, Dios mío". Por ejemplo, "Hija de tu madre, ¿no tiene vergüenza?!" cuando salía de casa sin sostén o cuando era más joven y no me gustaba banarmé (por cierto, ¿por qué los niños odian tanto banarsé?). La traducción directa es simplemente hija de tu madre. Me han dicho innumerables veces que mi madre y yo nos parecemos mucho, específicamente mi hermano, específicamente cuando ella y yo peleamos. Guerreras fogosas y testarudos que hacen todo por amor, incluso cuando no vemos que nos estamos apretando demasiado.

Me fue de Nueva York hace ocho años atrás, pero cada vez que vuelvo a casa me reciben con rosas y frutas recién cortadas. Sábanas nuevas en la cama y el ventilador o la calefacción ya instalados porque sabe que siempre tengo demasiado calor o demasiado frío. Es una ternura, un tipo dulce de amor que a veces se olvida cuando las llamadas telefónicas terminan abruptamente o entre lágrimas. Las discusiones ocurren con menos frecuencia ahora, pero cuando lo hacen, creo que es porque ambos nos aferramos a sueños de cuentos de hadas. Ella deseaba que yo fuera un doctor temeroso de Dios, casado y probablemente con dos hijos ahora. Y yo deseando que ella me viera como soy.

Atrevida significa ballsy en español. Otro dicho común con el que mi madre me corona suavemente. Siempre me río cuando me mira de reojo cuando le cuento mis aventuras. Cuando me quedo un poco tarde en Brooklyn, cuando hago viajes solo o simplemente hago una caminata solo. Atrevida. La mujer que traspasó fronteras, la primera de nueve. Vino aquí sin dinero y sin caras conocidas. Ella me cuenta las historias de su supervivencia. Encontró su camino desde Los Ángeles, a Oakland, a Reno, y eventualmente a Brooklyn. Madre soltera que logró mantener las luces encendidas para dos niños. Estudió conmigo noche y día para su ciudadanía. Se convirtió en dueño de una propiedad. Hizo su propio negocio a partir de su amor por la cocina. Desafió todas las probabilidades. Atrevida. Como dije, mi madre y yo nos parecemos mucho.

Mi madre encontró el Cristianismo más adelante en su vida y durante un tiempo ella y yo asistíamos juntos a los servicios varias veces por semana durante años. Sé que ella se aferra a la esperanza de que yo regresaré al camino de servidor diligente que alguna vez fui. Quiere desesperadamente que escriba sobre Dios. Y, en muchos sentidos, lo a he hecho, pero no en la luz que ella esperaba.

Este libro está plagado de historias de nuestra relación y de nuestra religión que alguna vez compartimos. Historias de mi identidad. Historias de dolor de mi propio pasado, por el de mis comunidades. Historias de amor y alegría triunfando en las situaciones más improbables. Cada parte de mi vida está recubierta de su esencia, ya sea directa o indirectamente.

I. EL EPIRITU SANTO
(the holy spirit)

Flesh gives birth to flesh, but the Spirit gives birth to Spirit.
John 3:6

Landay #1[1]

And I hold tightly to your sweet love.

The one that pulled me from my grave before the dirt came.

<hr>

[1] A Landay is a form of poetry formed in Afghanistan. Landay origins come from girls and women who were barred from reading and writing, so to pass on information, they would memorize these Landays and carry them to the next person's ears. They are rooted in themes of love and grief. I whisper these to a mother who loves me dearly and does not know how to love me (w)holy.

code-switch

Growing up with a Latin New Yorker tongue,
        public school in the hood tongue,
                my neighbors were in gangs tongue,
                        my first kiss was an MS-13 tongue.

I never knew what a code switch was.
        I didn't know my *dead-ass* and
                it's brick needed explaining.

Until my 2nd-grade teacher tells me
        gunna is not a word.

Until I heard the other honors kids
        talk and realize I may be doing something wrong.

Until my roommate tells me "oh,
        I've always known it to be easier this way".

I sit within myself
        and question my entire vocabulary -
                Buggin', OD, Guap, Hooptie,
                        Bumblefuck Nowhere,

and nowhere did I learn there was a
        different dictionary for professionalism.

When I started working in offices, I began
        collecting the
                "correct" translation
                        of my
                                first language.

Buggin' became
        "John was very out of line for that".

OD became
        "Could you please calm down?"

Bumblefuck Nowhere became
> "Wow, I've never heard of Osgood, Idaho before! What's it like?"

I quickly realized my dialect smelled of
> Chicharones con tostones
>> you get from the bodega
>>> on 83rd st.

And when I say it only comes out when
> I'm drunk
>> I mean -

I'm fucking lit right now
Dressed head to toe in Baby Phat
While Bobby Valentino plays in the background…

"I've always known
> it to be easier this way,"
>> my roommate with promotions
>>> I've never seen.

My peers suited up with 6 figure homes.
> They knew there was a game to be played
>> in the system we call America, it's called "Assimilate".

Some traded their golden hoops
> for silver studs. Curls straightened out
>> by the kindest Dominican lady
>>> with the meanest hands.

And I look at them with love.
> What we do to survive.
>> The pressure to cover up…

You good?
Yeah - yeah
I'm good.

Bangalore, India | April 2024

I. In Bangalore, the most common mode of transportation is some type of motorbike.

II. In most cases, there will be more than one person on it, upwards of four if the children are small enough to fit, maybe not comfortably, but fit.

III. If it is two men, the one riding in the back will hold his hands anywhere besides the driver's hips or waist. They will interlock their fingers behind them, on top of their helmet, or crossed arms across their chest. The seatbelt of safety that is the driver is non-existent. They are hot lava body.

IV. While, on the other hand, the women embrace each other. Tenderly. Sisterly. Perhaps as lovers. It's on a case-by-case basis.

V. They rest their heads on the backs, on the shoulders of Sarees and scarves floating in the wind of bumpy roads. Arms securely wrap around the abdomen of their guide.

VI. I imagine us in different worlds - in one, under the safety of our femininity grabbing waists, sneaking kisses on backs.

VII. In another, fighting the temptation to do the same as men.

VIII. In another where we can chameleon ourselves, one feminine, one masculine, masking our queerness to be more palpable in a place where faggotry does not seem allowed.

IX. In all, we hold each other, on the bike, in the park, or in the comfort of our bed.

The Captain

At White Horse, I met
        The Captain.
An older Butch with a heavy hand
        for Whiskey (read: medicine).
They look at my camera,
        ask if it takes 35mm.
I flash them the film canister,
        locked in the back of its cage.
They smile tenderly & for a moment
        I'm invited in to see their history.
The young Captain, with a camera
        slightly weighing down their neck.
In my heart, the Captain has always fearlessly
        been out of the closet.
They've always had the same buzzcut, less greyed
        and more ashy blonde.
They skip towards me with a sing-songy tone
        Nanccccccyyyyyy.
Check in hand with a sweet wink that
        tells me I see you.
And in another world, The Captain and I are in the
        80s.
Them, bartender, while I'm still the patron,
        with my hand on the thigh of
the person next to me,
        hungry in a space where being
gay is allowed to be all consumed.
        The Captain wore leather as their
uniform; I'm sure of it. And we smoked cigarettes
        and the straights would be scared of us;
I'm sure of it. I'm sure that we would laugh at the
        too-chicken-shit of a person who
thinks hurling *Dykes!* at us would change who we are.
        The Captain, a lighthouse sent
in the flash of a moment when I feared there were
        no elders around me I could learn from.

I Pledge Allegiance To

I landed on the cliffside of Big Sur and was caught by the ankle, upside down, staring at a ceiling of millions of stars. I twist my neck, bending at the edge to meet the moon. Here, I should be petrified at the deafening silence and the unknown - the ghosts that scale up to potentially find me but instead my fear lies in the comfort of my own home. Between me and tiny screens, I hear stories of my kin's life on the line or life in mourning. I hear the stories of the bills that passed and those that didn't. A record number a record number a record numb -

510

- I see myself in the mirror of the youth, the fervent, and the mighty. I pledge allegiance to them. Allegiance to the kids who didn't have the chance to be kids long enough. Who were forced into the life of adulthood because this world knows in order to crush the spirit you have to kill the kid. Kids - I pledge allegiance to you.

The butch in the smoking section calls me a breath of fresh air and

burden melts away from my shoulders.
A smoker's lungs in need of oxygen
and I, a breath of fresh air.

They leave and come back to find me
seated where they left me. And this is
less a meet-cute and more found-family.

And we talk about families, work,
and how I don't have a type but if they
remind me of a cowboy, I'm along for the ride.

And I ride that high of the hot butch who
felt familiar on the balcony of the Palladium
between drags of a borrowed cigarette

on days that waking up does not
feel like enough. On the days I forget that
there aren't only embers shining inside me

but a whole fucking lighthouse where
refuge can be found in intimate one-night
pleasantries between you and

the butch in the smoking section.

Field Notes on Birds

I.   On hikes through valleys and meadows and dark forest floors, the ominous feeling of being alone can overtake the body. And then - a song.

II.   The siren sound of a Spotted Towhee, foraging the damp Redwood grounds as I strip off the unexpectedly-too-warm jacket packed for this November expedition. Finding relief in this tiny thing that would not be able to protect me from our shared apex predator,

III.   loneliness - Towhees are known to love for life. They pick up nesting materials to build a home with the one they'll yoke the increasingly cold California Winters with.

IV.   I only recently began sleeping in the middle of my bed.

V.   Saving a space for you longer than we were together. I dreamed of a Redwood wedding - saw it clear as day.

VI.   I only recently realized I was the only one dreaming.

VII.   Towhees are known to love for life. I wonder if they are known to experience heartbreak?

VIII.   Can a Towhee love so deeply that it forgets itself?

IX.   Does it lose its white spots, no longer able to dance for another lover when the one they had dies?

X.   Does the Towhee also lay on the damp Redwood floor, in mourning, paralyzed in grief?

Nancy Azcona (b. 1995)
Rothko, 2024

Times New Roman on Google Sheet

Have you ever seen a Rohtko piece in person?
Neither have I.

I was told once that seeing them on a screen wasn't enough.
I was told that the purpose of a Rothko is to be faced with the
Goliath-sized waves of reds, and blacks, and blues.
To be devoured by erupting emotions.

Have you ever seen someone you loved drowning?
Neither have I.

But the tiniest town of people have seen me nearly suffocate.
My body, the artwork of near blistering red from boiling water
shower falls and scratches to escape the very skin I was in.
My body, embodies the solemnness associated with blue
and black behind my eyes.

Have you been consumed by the Goliath that is someone you love
moving about this world ruled by their pain, fueled by
the cruelness shown to them? Devastating.

To be the Rothko.
        And to be its witness.

AN OBITUARY TO THE INNOCENT

TORNILLO, TX, GAZA, SUDAN, AMERICA — (REDACTED), AS YOUNG AS A FEW MONTHS OLD, DIED TODAY, (INSERT THE DATE TODAY HERE), AT (LOCATION), FOLLOWING THE CARELESS HATRED FROM THEIR OWN GOVERNMENT.

El Salvador Views from Secretary Mel Martinez Visit [Electronic Record]; Photographs Documenting the Secretary's Headquarters and Field Activities, and Agency Officials and Events, between 2001–2014; Records of the National Archives Catalog

The Children -

They are survived by no one. Fathers, mothers, siblings, friends, the school they once ran around in, and their favorite teddy bears' whereabouts are unknown. They were not found under the rubble. They are buried behind the prison, unnamed. They've been separated for years in kennels like impounded dogs.

(NAME) was born and raised in Oaxaca, Gaza, Central Africa, Tornillo, TX, and is the child of (REDACTED) and (REDACTED). (UNIDENTIFIED CHILDREN) didn't have a chance to live anywhere besides the place where they were unjustly buried. They never settled down. They never had children of their own.

Angelic La Moose, whose grandfather was a Flathead chief, wearing costume her mother made; full-length, standing, in front of a tent, Flathead Reservation, Montana [Electronic Record]; General Photographs of Indians, between 1900–1957; Records of the National Archives Catalog

Before the airstrikes, (UNIDENTIFIED CHILDREN), most were set to live fulfilling lives. We are certain they had dreams they never had a chance to live out. Before the encampment, we presume, they knew innocence. We presume they knew unfiltered joy. Before Presidents removed their names and replaced them with a numerical placard, we presume, they were proud to be an American, born one or not.

(UNIDENTIFIED CHILDREN) could not have imagined a life short-lived. They deserved to be alive today. (UNIDENTIFIED CHILDREN) will be missed by all who knew them.

Visiting hours are plastered on every social media app at (YOUR BEDROOM), and the funeral will be held at (UNMARKED BURIAL GROUNDS), every day, until the end of time. There will be a reception following.

Pawn Shop Victory

The Father, an older Armenian
man speaks in tongues, Russian
one moment and Arabic the next.
He sits me down and inspects
the ring with an eyeglass.
The Son buzzed me in while someone
sat confessing, I waited my turn.
He blesses me with mournful eyes
as I pull out my sachet of other golds.
I can tell by his smile that I
have nothing of importance. It is
Sunday, and my church has
bulletproof glass and an iron
gate. The scripture
on the walls are vintage gibsons,
I can hear them sing a cold and
broken *Hallelujah.*
(Hallelujah)
Sitting in the room of reconciliation,
I hear feet scutter around me.
I grew up hearing
God works hard but the Devil works harder
Wait no -
God works hard, but the love
of strangers works harder
or
God works, but the Holy Spirit is
the stranger next door.
The Holy Spirit
saw me tremble as I pulled out my wallet
that held cigarettes, hoping I did not drop
all of my dirty in this house of worship.
With kind eyes and a sense of family,
she taps my shoulders and hands me a 20,
baptizes me with a *Merry Christmas*
and disappears. It is Sunday and
I am weeping at the pulpit before
the Father, the Son, and the Holy Spirit.

It is Sunday, and I'm giving my priest
a ring that was given to me in the name
of matrimony. It is Sunday and
my church today is a pawn shop on
the corner of Victory and Magnolia.

Ortolan Ritual

They say to wear a veil over your face
when consuming an Ortolan. It keeps in
the aromas of the Armagnac it drowned in.
It keeps your shame hidden from God as you
eat the innocent. Feet first, you stuff the songbird
into your mouth, all but the beak, savor the
plumpness of the roast, and spit out the bones.

Inhumane.
    Delicacy.

~~They say to~~ wear a veil ~~over your face~~
when consuming ~~an Ortolan. It keeps in~~
the ~~aromas of the Armagnac it drowned in.~~
~~It keeps your~~ shame ~~hidden from God~~ as you
eat the innocent. ~~Feet~~ first, you stuff ~~the songbird~~
into your mouth, ~~all but the beak,~~ savor the
plumpness ~~of the roast, and~~ spit out the bones.

~~Inhumane.~~
    Delicacy.

Divine Reckoning

I
Stuck in limbo before.

II
Stuck in limbo before
Minos wraps his tail around
my body 10 times.
I would stay here if I were
to be damned with you.

III
Stuck in limbo before
Minos wraps his tail around
my body 10 times.
I would stay here if I were
to be damned with you.
Eve, chin fruit-soaked in gluttony
for the knowledge of what it is to be a God.

IIII
Stuck in limbo before
Minos wraps his tail around
my body 10 times.
I would stay here if I were
to be damned with you.
Eve, chin fruit-soaked in gluttony
for the knowledge of what it is to be a God.
The glint of hoarded gold between
my teeth, I tuck away my greed.

V
Stuck in limbo before
Minos wraps his tail around
my body 10 times.
I would stay here if I were
to be damned with you.
Eve, chin fruit-soaked in gluttony
for the knowledge of what it is to be a God.
The glint of hoarded gold between
my teeth, I tuck away my greed
under my tongue like Communion.
Confess my sins to the cold concrete.

VI
Stuck in limbo before
Minos wraps his tail around
my body 10 times.
I would stay here if I were
to be damned with you.
Eve, chin fruit-soaked in gluttony
for the knowledge of what it is to be a God.
The glint of hoarded gold between
my teeth, I tuck away my greed
under my tongue like Communion.
Confess my sins to the cold concrete,
fingers crossed behind my back as I bow
to the altar. You are no longer my religion,
my prayer - lips, flower-pressed whispers into the
scars of my body.

VII
Stuck in limbo before
Minos wraps his tail around
my body 10 times.
I would stay here if I were
to be damned with you.
Eve, chin fruit-soaked in gluttony
for the knowledge of what it is to be a God.
The glint of hoarded gold between
my teeth, I tuck away my greed
under my tongue like Communion.
Confess my sins to the cold concrete,
fingers crossed behind my back as I bow
to the altar. You are no longer my religion,
my prayer - lips, flower-pressed whispers into the
scars of my body. The slaughter of
all of the selves I've left behind
beg me to walk the righteous path.

VIII
Stuck in limbo before
Minos wraps his tail around
my body 10 times.
I would stay here if I were
to be damned with you.
Eve, chin fruit-soaked in gluttony
for the knowledge of what it is to be a God.
The glint of hoarded gold between
my teeth, I tuck away my greed
under my tongue like Communion.
Confess my sins to the cold concrete,
fingers crossed behind my back as I bow
to the altar. You are no longer my religion,
my prayer - lips, flower-pressed whispers into the
scars of my body. The slaughter of
all of the selves I've left behind
beg me to walk the righteous path.
There are years lost to my crookedness
of playing pretend. Pretend that I am
good in all the godly ways.

IX
Stuck in limbo before
Minos wraps his tail around
my body 10 times.
I would stay here if I were
to be damned with you.
Eve, chin fruit-soaked in gluttony
for the knowledge of what it is to be a God.
The glint of hoarded gold between
my teeth, I tuck away my greed
under my tongue like Communion.
Confess my sins to the cold concrete,
fingers crossed behind my back as I bow
to the altar. You are no longer my religion,
my prayer - lips, flower-pressed whispers into the
scars of my body. The slaughter of
all of the selves I've left behind
beg me to walk the righteous path.
There are years lost to my crookedness
of playing pretend. Pretend that I am
good in all the godly ways.
Go ahead, feed me to Lucifer.
Indeed, I am
a sinner.

II. EL HIJO
(the son)

A wise man brings joy to his father,
but a foolish son brings grief to his mother.
Proverbs 10:1

Landay #2

Mother, I hear your cries across lands.

Does the sound of my world drenched in happiness hurt you?

Ring Three Times

My mother calls me and I ignore it.
      My mother calls me and I ignore it.
            My mother calls and the phone is upstairs
                  like my body knew I would hesitate to pick
                  it up anyways, to save me from the
                  guilty reality that I would just ignore it.

I inherited a pre-disposition to
      take care of my caretaker.
            My mother calls me and I already know
                  how the conversation is going to go.
                  I tell my therapist I don't know how much
                  more I have left in me to tell my mother
                  that she can live in two worlds.

The one where she sacrificed everything for us.
      And the one where she becomes Abraham.
            Abraham - The Father of Many Nations.
                  He heard the whispers of what he needed to do
                  to be a good servant. A good servant.
                  Carried Issac. Bound Issac. Lifted a knife to Issac.

I am bound by the knowledge that my mother
      hates the sinner. Wants to dig a dagger from
            sternum to stomach to resurrect the child she bore
                  in her own womb. This is godliness to her.
                  To pray for her child to live a life where they lie
                        to themselves for the comfort of the podium.

And I so desperately wish I could give her
      the child she imagines me to still be.
            Last Saturday I sang in a church.
                  Do you think she would believe me?
                  I sang in a church for the first time in over 10 years.
                  I was the child she always wanted me to be.

Singing in the church in a circle of queer freaks.
As a tenor with nearly two years of T in me.
Do you think she would still bind my hands?
Do you think she would still
hold a knife to my heart
if she could hear me singing -

Holy breath, and holy name
Will you ease, will you ease this pain?

Are You There God? It's Me, Nancy[5]

On Sunday, in a beaten-down yellow school bus, on our way to learn about
  God, I showed another person my poetry. I was 13 and depression had just
begun to nestle beside me every night. She sat quietly, unsure how she landed in
the role of therapist, and said, "Why don't we write about loving God instead?".

At 16, I read my poetry from a pulpit.
At 16, I was prophesied to tell stories that would free the burdened.
At 16, I unloaded my burden into the nearest toilet bowl.
At 16, I kissed a girl on a dare and cried.
At 16, I prayed. And prayed. And prayed.
At 16, I undressed. And undressed. And undressed.
At 16, I was all pink lacy bra and webcams while men masturbated.
At 16, I sang in the church band.
At 16, I counted 101 pills to see how many it would take to swallow me whole.
At 16, a man named Ryan swallowed me whole.
At 16, I saw my rapist for the first time in 8 years, in church.
At 16, I asked my mother for forgiveness for being defiled.
At 16, I pantomimed on stage for hundreds of disciples.
At 16, I begged my brother not to burn in hell.
At 16, I wrote poems I would not read from the pulpit.
At 16, I wrote. And wrote. And wrote.

Writing - waiting to see if God will ever write about loving me instead.

---

[5]　　The church taught how to be a good Martyr. Taught me to shed myself if needing
a reason to live other than Jesus himself, I do not think they expected me to be a Martyr
for love. A Martyr for children who suffer. A Martyr for those in my community who need
a hand to hold while they pass on.

Are You There Nancy? It's Me, God.

Sundays are branded in you as the day of worship.
You've traded church services for rituals.

For an altar that holds dead things, to talk to the dead.
Palo santo, water enchanted by the moon, a branch from Death Valley.

On Sundays, you sit across your window and light 3
candles. Ignite rosemary, leave it ablaze until -

whoosh - smoke trickles up and I see the baptism of
clearing energies and hear your invocation:
    Dear Father who art in heaven   I call for you every day and ask to
    please forgive this sinner,   deliver me from my past, one full of false prophets.
Most of the time you feel a rush of heat. Rarely, a voice clear as day.
I've sent you your grandparents. Your aunts and uncles.

Your friends who loved you like you shared the same blood.
On Sundays, you read to them. You spend time catching them up.

You make a purpose to honor your elders in a way that cannot be taught.
For this, I am proud. For this, I know I taught you well.

And you wrote wondering where I have been. Questioning all of my love for you.
For this, I have failed you. For this, I am sorry.

one day

im writing
and reading
a lot and yet
and yet
not enough
turn to soil
to jumping in
puddles to
laughter to
play dress up
draw lines
on my face
call it art
call myself
art // *art*
ive fallen
in deep
deep
love
of the person
in the mirror
even in their
grief
they are
beautiful
hold their
anger
tenderly
far from
fragile and
yet porcelain
in calloused
palms
ask to
be held
while they
hold others
stories

hold others
grief
dont know
how
to not
even when
they
have no
more space
in their
hands for
spare
skeleton keys
one day
there will
be time
to put it
all down
one day
there will
be time to
cry it all out
one day
there will be
one day

Someday I'll Love Romeo

After claire schwartz after ocean voung after frank o'hara

Romeo, open your eyes. Put both hands in front of you.
Hold the healing spirit between   each   open   space,

find mirrors in still puddles, and be a witness.
Burly and beautiful, look: you can see
your grandfather's eyes staring back.

You hold his name tucked under your tongue
for safekeeping but hold it between your teeth to show
your mother that his sweetness still lives on.

Uncage your voice, let it echo
through the ears of ghosts you once held
close. You loved the haunting, the witching hour,
the time between 3 and 6am when you transformed.

Magic being, you alchemized into Love after
you thought there was no love to be had.

Romeo, you are *always* in the room where there
is love to be had. Child of Change.
Don't dismiss the bloodline that runs deep in you.

Tenderness can only be known through
the warrior's palms. You've bound freedom
and fight together in a constrictor knot,

and you know not of what decadent life lies
before you: a life of worship and rest, liberation,
honey jar joy. Each new day, a Sunday.

Romeo, it's okay to be
frightened of the unknown.

Painfully aware of patterns of heartache and
how your body can only take so much more.

Boxeador, one day you will be able to retire your
gloves. People will stop betting on you,
they will stop yelling at you from the stands.

Burial is not the only means to solace.
One day, the burden of what-ifs will melt off of you,
the lightness will feel like you have lost the weight
of several generations' transgressions.

Nancy Romeo Frenesy Azcona,
you will do more than just survive.
You will live.

You. Will. Live.

Needles Needles

A Guide To Your Treatment

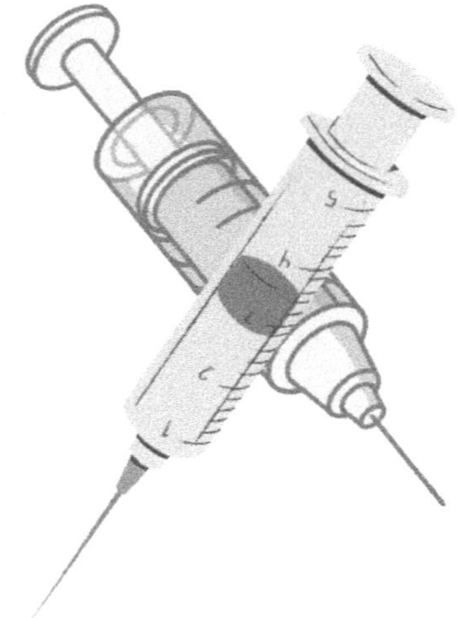

What is Psoriasis?

In order to get diagnosed and
treated for (psoriasis)
blue scrubs with matching
gloves and masks must take a
piece of you and leave you with
an open wound that will close
to just be another scar
on your body.

This will be your first biopsy.

What is Testosterone?

One day you will write a letter
to those you love the most.
You will sob a painful sob, gasp
for air, and think this is it.

Think, I've made it far enough.

Think, I'm sorry I couldn't live to
see you fall in love.

The next day, you will call
Planned Parenthood. You will
ask to consult with someone to
start taking Testosterone.

Wait for a month until they can
see you. Go in and get shown
how to puncture your body
with a 1.5-inch needle.

How Long Do You Have To Take Both?

For the medicine to ward off the scaly
skin that aches and drives you mad you
are required to take it once

every 3 months. For the rest of your life.
This one is half an inch. Smaller and less
often. You accept the terms and
conditions.

They say the medicine to ward off the
feelings of not being enough
to live in your own body you are
required to take it for as long as

needed. You can up and/or lower the
dosage as you see fit. Must get
blood work done to make sure
everything else is up to code.

You are told by your first doctor, there is
a range to be in to match the man
you may want to become, but the most
important part is that you feel

good in the newness of this body. You
will be unsure what that looks
like at first but it will become obvious
like the dry achy patches of skin
disappearing.

When new hairs and voice changes
appear, you will know what it feels like to come
home.

NA, 27, Online Now ●

i fear that i will never be man enough
when on Grindr i get called goddess
and queen say pussy and fuck i bet you can
really take it and testing the waters and
ive only been with women before
so i find home in the womaness of your pink
and it scares me when you are 900ft away
because youre too close to the truth that
my whole life ive felt like an experiment
ive felt like the stepping stone to so many hugh
jackman realities so just fuck me til i moan
like your favorite pornstar til i win
the academy award for cumming on command
and i cant even remember
the names of the men whove seen my body
men who know me by the color of my nipples
sex doesnt mean you love me
but at least i know you like me enough
to fuck me and i've cried over guys
that didn't know what a caprese salad was
and i know that seems silly
but i made this salad with homegrown basil so
fuck him and ive cried over a man who
softly kissed my hands as if to say i love you but
my everything wasnt enough so fuck him,
and maybe one day if i stay long enough
the gay boy of my dreams will buy me a drink
or bump into me at my favorite bookstore
saying all the right things at all the right times
who will be more than okay with my
flamboyancy and wont mistake it
for divine femininity because of
my lack of top surgery and maybe
i dont know what i want
i run in cycles of 4-year long
self-building binges
a constant catching

of myself a constant
relearning of myself
and i know all things
end so im asking
to just let
the heart
break
en-

i mean, hi :), yeah i'm still up :)

SCREENPLAY: DON'T PICK UP THE PHONE[3]

INT.   NANCY'S BEDROOM - MID-DAY ON JULY 4TH

July 4th is, ironically, one of Nancy's favorite holidays. They aren't tied to the sentiment of American Freedom™, but rather tied to all the time they've spent with loved ones over BBQ, drinks, and the glitz and glam of fireworks. Every year, they're transported to, driving into Boston after a whole work shift at Sephora and seeing the fireworks go off on their way north. Or the one where they almost got stranded in the middle of the ocean in San Diego. Or where they're in an intense game of Spoons, in someone's concrete backyard, sweaty, competitive, and full of love.

Nancy is sitting on their bed, a little high, with no plans on the Patriotic holiday for the first time in years. Not thinking much of it, they lay in the mounds of pillows they've carefully curated, reading their 3rd book of the month when a voice message from their mother suddenly awakens their phone's screen. Nancy looks puzzled, having not spoken to their mother in a few weeks. She decides to listen.

> MAMI
> (Intense sobbing, with an undertone of anger)
> …Siempre soñé con llevar a mi hija al altar.

Nancy did not hear the whole thing before they were outside of their body. Within the first 30 seconds, they knew not to listen all the way through but they did anyway. They are stoic in their bed, cross-legged, phone in hand, looking ahead with a soft gaze as if trying not to fall asleep.

> MAMI
> (Intense sobbing, with an undertone of anger)
> …y lo haré, porque eres mi **HIJA**, eres una **NIÑA**.

---

3   She is trying. In her own way, I think she is trying to be the mother I needed her to be.

Each proclamation over Nancy like daggers dug into their sternum. As their mother increases their prayer like vitriol at them, they too grow in anger.

CUT TO:

INT. NANCY'S BEDROOM - EVENING - A MONTH AND ½ LATER

It is a weekday and Nancy is getting ready for bed. Like clockwork, they are on their back with Maya Angelou's *I Know Why the Caged Bird Sings* grasped in between their thumb and pinky finger. It's been an exhausting month. Even though their card pulls for August told them not to be driven by emotion, they fully let themself get carried away with anxieties.

They are tired most nights, nervous system shot. They try to sustain themselves. They army crawl their way into normalcy most days. Receive critiques of their work, forget to answer emails for weeks, promise to set up catch-ups but never commit to a date. They are unlike themselves, but no one needs to know. And then - their phone screen lights up.

MAMABEAR flashes across the screen.

They watch the incoming call and debate. It's been a few weeks, and they don't feel like getting into an argument. It is 9 at night, but guilt pangs at their heart. They haven't been able to have a conversation with their mother since coming out that doesn't make them feel like a disappointment. It's not a feeling anymore, actually. Nancy knows they are a disappointment to her.

They hesitate one more second.

Then, they answer.

                    NANCY
          (quietly so as to not awaken their roommates)
     Hola mamí.

48

                    MAMI
              (with melancholy)
         Hola.

There is something most migrant moms are masters at,
being the only person in the world who has suffered. The
second part of their mastery: never letting you forget
it.

The conversation progresses as expected - full of Facebook-
esque Christian quotes and no real acknowledgment of
what has occurred. It's a volley of a mother being
cryptic and judgmental with a thin veil of love and a
child tired of their mother's illusion of love.

                    NANCY
              (annoyed)
         ¿Cuando me llamas, de esto
         siempre vamos a hablar?

                    MAMI
              (annoyed)
         Yo no sé…

And Nancy can't help but laugh. Their mother, when in
an argument, reverts to arguing like a teenager who was
just told they were grounded.

Aloof, annoyed, and a bit of an asshole. You're not
supposed to say your mother is acting like an asshole,
but it does not negate the behavior.

*I don't know. I don't know if I'll ever accept you.
I don't know that I won't keep hurting you. I don't
know how to be a different mother. I don't know how to
separate my hurt from yours. I don't know if I'll ever
see this as anything but selfish. I don't know if I can
grow anymore. I don't know. I don't know. I don't know.
I don't know if I'll ever stop trying to ~~convince guilt
change hate who you are make you whole again~~ love you.*

On The Other Side

I was on.

the other side of the mirror, blank-faced, gnashing my teeth, blood pouring out of me. My feet firmly planted in Valley Village. I saw myself deteriorate. Waste away to 9 AM Gatorade disguised Gin cocktails. Just a little drink. Just a little drink. Just a little drink. Drink. Drink. Drunk. Drunken mess. Hard to black out now ain't it? You know the routine, two, three fingers down your throat. Secret shots down the hatch. Raw throat. *It would be easy to give in to it.* You said it yourself. It's in your blood. This is your endowment. Thank your father. Thank your father. Thank you Father. I'm drinking the body by the bottle. The harvest of fermented grapes, my sacrament of healing. Stained red lips tell my confessions before I even have a chance to sit in the seat of penitents. I disguise it well. My cheeks are still plump with an emptied stomach and veins full of distilled rye. I've convinced myself that the feeling of nothing is better than the feeling of everything. I would've stayed convinced. Some days I don't know which one is best. Feeling numb. Feeling everything. Death certain whichever way. For now - I've stopped. Stopped the glassy eyed version of myself sinking my teeth further into flesh. Stopped the car from careening over the unfinished road that

I was on

III. EL PADRE
(the father or the parent)

All things have been handed over to me by my Father, and no one knows the Son except the Father, and no one knows the Father except the Son and anyone to whom the Son chooses to reveal him.
Matthew 11:27

Landay #3

I know you like the prayers in my palms.

I hold your grief, ma, puedes sostener el mío?

Baptism for The Unholy

Drown me. / Kill me / off. / Pour the / Holy / water down my / throat. / Make me / dedicate the rest of my days to / something / unseen. / Make me / carry / Guilt / in my / Heart. / Make me / Lie / to my mother. / Hide my / anger / when she / mourns for the / fallen sons. / One / pedophile / the other / Gay. / Both / Sinners / in the eye of the / beholder. / The beholder / my mother. / The Miscreant / Me. / Queer / as a / 3 dollar bill. / She says / *praying for a husband.* / I write / prayers / between the lips / of my / hookup. / I consummate an / Unholy / marriage. / Do not / speak / of my / lovers / to my mother. / Tacit. / There's / no way / she does / not / know. / I do not / hide. / The closet / burnt / down. / But there is a / pool. / Full of her / dreams / for me. / They involve / a husband. / And children. / I do not know if I want / children / with a / husband. / Those are her dreams. / So, / I kill / parts of / me / until one day / the chimera-filled basin / empties / to no longer / Drown me.

Reliquias de Un Madre y Su Hija

Our heirlooms are stories, recipes, a pair of gold earrings, a few Polaroids of grandparents
I barely knew.

Recipes of Pupusas that take days to make
and Sopa de Res served on a hot summer day.
Big hoop earrings paired with dark brown lipstick
and the whitest jeans I've ever seen.
Stories of a *coyote* who brought her safely to *los angeles*.
A photo of her comedian father with so much more life
he didn't get a chance to live.
My mother with a knotted throat -

Mi viejito, mi viejito.

En los años pasados me han faltado
recuerdos que nunca existieron.
No tengo estas historias de cuando me
crecí con un abuelo que me hizo reír hasta llorar.
Ni de un abuelo que me dio consejos
contra los hombres que abusaron
de quienes llevabancorazones
más grandes que la cruz.
No tengo nadie a quien llamar
Mi viejito -

I fear that I will not have new stories *de mi viejito.*
They will live in this liminal space
where my father would come home
from a long day of work
and I would take off his boots
so we could eat dinner together.
Arroz con gandules y guineo,
watching Pacquiao with Tio Náo
in my makeshift living room bedroom.
The stories of where my father tried to be a father.

I will speak of my *viejita* and the days she tried to be a father.
And how the heirlooms she holds within her are stories -
The one of cocola y ubas *(Surviving)*.
The one where she climbed trees so high to shake the
green mangoes free from their vines *(Living)*.
The one about how she met my dad *(Surviving)*.
The one where she rests *(Dying)*.

Cuando yo pienso de mi herencia,
la cual yo pasare a los ninos de mi vida,
yo miro a mis vinilos y el libro
defotos que tengo
de todos losdias
de risa y musica que yo ha vivido.
Pienso del oro de mi mama y mi abuela
Pienso de las historias -
Las de los amores *(vivendo)*.
Las de mis vientes *(sobreviviendo)*.
cuando ella me acepta *(la muerte)*.

Camel Crush // Malboro Reds

Summer
        Time
                Cigarette my vices
                        mirror the
                Ones of
        my father.
And I buy a
        pack of
                menthols
                        Like
        It's my birthright
And California
        Banned my birthright
        so
It's like prohibition
                I
                Ask the
                        Liquor store clerk to see their
                Case of options and whisper
        into a dandelion of prayer
"Do you have any *other* cigarettes?"
                And there is a backroom.
                                And there are security cameras.
                And he could've asked me if I was a cop.
And I'm glad I don't look like a cop.
                And I'm led to my
                        security blankets of
                Camel
                Crushes.
You know the type that has
        the tiny vessel
                that you crunch
                        in
                between
        your teeth,
    or in between
your thumbs
        the way you try to pulverize

the fact that you do
in fact
have a father
that just
does not
care.
The doctor
asks me if I smoke,
and I tell her yes.
Tell her but not really.
I mention I buy maybe
2-3 packs
a year.
And is it a vice
if I use it sparingly.
If I use it on open
highways only?
Can a vice simply
be called a vice by the virtue
of inheritance?
When does my smoking
make me look more like
my father?
When does drinking
make me look like
my father?
The first time I saw him
drunk beyond belief,
I was 5.
Wailing at the fun house mirror
reflection of who I could be.
Warped and distorted,
I think I saw a graveyard.
I think I saw a treachery of ravens.
I think I saw a scythe
waiting to hug me.

inocencia perdida[4]

If I were re-born a
thing,
I would be metals
smithed
into a shield.
What I mean is,
there was not one
waking moment in
my childhood
that I did not need
to protect myself,
my mother's feelings,
the sanity of my family.
The last time my mother
struck my brother I was 8.
I, tiny tugger, begging
for the fight to stop.
The only voice
of reason in a
house full of adults.
How does one
regain their innocence
when they were born
with responsibilities.
My mother tells me
stories of playground
gossip. Other
caretakers' concerns
of how quiet I was.
¿Está bien?
¿Qué le pasa a tu hija?
And my prideful
mother would
defend me as
just being a
good kid.

---

[4]   I know what it is to be riddled with fear of losing someone you love so dearly to damnation; the church is good at that. I hold empathy for my mother while the child in me is also asking to be picked up - and between the two, most of the time, I choose my mother, as I always have.

My first
memory is
at 4 years old.
It was about
a fight.
A fight about me.
I remember a Princess
Jasmine doll and
a Toyota Corolla.
I remember
a fight for me.
I asked
what would happen
with all my clothes.
Te compraré
unos nuevos.
I remember a
fight about who
deserved to take
me. And I remember
my tiny hands.
The cassette player
I could see in the
back seat.
But most of all
I remember
the fight.
How fire can
take and burn
years of
recollections
in just a moment.
I knew even then
that I never
could become
friends with my
anger.

Altar For The Living
After Body Tracks, 1974 - Ana Mendieta

And I smear
my red on
white baptism
lace
so I can otherwise
contain
what I want
to say -

*I'm
sorry for this*

That I'm begging
for the family
I was born into.
I've built an altar
for the living.
A Father who hasn't
called me in two years,
nephews and nieces
who no longer
know my name,
a brother who found
the aftermath of an
unsent suicide note.

I wish I could've
done more to help

you not feel
this way

My leaving was
necessary but
not a single hand landed
on my shoulder
to ask me

where in my heart
this haste lived.
I chose Lonely
instead of being given
lonely in the orphanhood
of my living family.

I wish
I could've
protected
you more

Car wheels turning
left and right
and left again.
Up mountains
and across seas,
across the same miles
my mother traveled.
Stuck in this labyrinth
of false homes.
I'm a feral dog
starved
seeking someone's
warmth as sustenance.
My incessant need
to be loved -
to become whole.

I won't know
how to
live

The only memory
I have
of being
a sibling
stays trapped

behind Polaroids.
I hate the silence
that falls
when I tell my
roommates
that they never
reach out.

We can't
leave
each other

Palo santo
smoke ripples up
on this California
winter morning.
I wash away the red-hot
heat that lives
upon my cheek
from the spiraling
thoughts of
last night's
pillow talk

In this
crazy
world

And still,
I am someone's
daughter
And someone's
sister
And someone's
aunt
And still,

Atrevida

Niña atrevida que   tu pensea

           hacer cuando el mundo

te enseña tiempo y   tiempo que no le gustan a las niñas

atrevidas.   Que vas aser cuando te tratan   a callar la voz tiempo

       y tiempo, te van a tratrar callar el voce.   Niña atrevida

ponte te q u e t a.   T r a n q u i l i s a t e.

       Ponte b o n i t a.   S o n r i a.   Que a los hombres le gustan.

Calmada.   Que le gustan.   C a l l a d a.   Que le gustan.

D e c a í d a.   Niña atrevida muéstrame tus ojos.

Quiero ver cuánto más dolor

           puedes sostener.

En esta vida te golpearána

          un centímetro de tu último

         s o p l o .

        Niña atrevida

         tenga

                    c u i d a d o.

What Daughters Come Down To[2]
After Patricia Smith

My mother does not know the heavy an only daughter carries, I'm sure.
The unseen, the forgotten, the songbird crooning a mournful hum,
while the others, soundless, receive a lifetime of *I love you too.*
Perfection, innocently forced upon me nestled in with God's
watchful eye, and yet - I wonder what it is to live in her bones.
One of Eight, competing for the shade from the heat of the
never-eclipsing sun. If her heart ever ached, do you wonder
if it was from the blistering burns of her own sons? She is
the strongest mountain God has ever formed, I wonder
if she knows I can feel her heavy. That her decision, day after day,
to keep her back upright does not go unnoticed. I recede into
myself knowing that day after day my efforts to not lose
the child she knows goes unnoticed. There is a boy inside of me screeching
to be let out. To bury the daughter that once was miles south
into deep earth, where even moss cannot grow. There are some
days I haul shame like it is my only cross to carry, overloading my spine
with the hopes of my mother's daughter, while my soul thirsts
for freedom from disappointment. I wonder if those
who defy their mother's womb get into heaven?
Anddoes the title of angel get ripped from our ribs, wings clipped?
I am hundreds of miles away, but I can see
her hand on her heart, hand covering her mouth, hand
and hand digging through soil, begging for the body to resurface.
I imagine mourning the living will be difficult. Matriarchy now draped
in a veil of abomination. I know the rain showers
that will haunt her. My mother, the fighter,
purpled by each blow of her daughter's insistent need
to find the god
inside. Her daughter
trying to find joy in the Spring of blooming
newness. *She will still love you,*
I think.

---

[2] I love my mother dearly. I see her and see a woman made of survival and others' sorrows. She tells me that when I was in her womb, she no longer wanted to live. That people would tell her to stay with my father until he gets out. That the prisoner's wife has a duty to uphold until the sentence is done. "It will serve you well", they told her. So she did, with me in her belly. I am convinced I absorbed the battles yet to come of living a life I did not want to live to make sure my duty is upheld.

Duplex on Land

After José Olivarez Ars Poetica line
Question: Is migration possible if there is no "other" land to arrive in?

Question: Is migration possible if there is no "other" land to arrive in?
Answer: My blood's blood is inherently a migrant's blood.

From El Salvador to Los Angeles there were trails of migrants' blood.
My mother crossed into lands not hers con un sueño, El Sueño Americano.

Question: Can you tell me, what is your *American Dream*?
Answer: To shed myself of everything that makes me American.

Violence spilling over in crimson red, does that make me American?
I bite the hand that feeds me, and weep when its boot meets my stomach -

Question: How many more innocent deaths can you stomach?
Answer: Please, do not make me look at the number.

Children locked in cages have their names replaced with a number.
Because those full of life are always for whom the bell tolls first -

Question: Greed or Power, which should go first?
Answer: They are the same, destroy them both.

The rocky mountains and my moms pueblo in Batres, can I love them both?
And that is the plight of being an immigrant in both lands.

Answer: No, because I've become an immigrant to all lands.
Question: Is migration possible if there is no "other" land to arrive in?

CI TI ZEN SH IP

after N.H. Pritchard

I
T EX T
M Y
M OT HER
T E
A MO
MU CH O
T E
E S T OY
M AN D AN DO
E ST O
P OR Q UE
G ENT E
A N
VI STO
IN MI GRA C IÓN
E N
B R ENT WO OD.
ICE has been spotted in my hometown where my friends were Dreamers,
where ESL classes came in abundance, where –
S OU N D ING
O UT
W OR DS
W AS
A
P RI V IL E GE
to us with white picket fence fantasies. As
N UE S TR O
PR I MOS
S OŃ A RON
D E
N UE S TRO
VI DAS.
My mother holds up her
CI TI ZEN SH IP
A F TER
S W EAR ING

H ER
L O YAL TY
TO
the red, white, and blue nearly
TH IR T EEN
Y EAR S
A GO.
Still, I send her a screenshot that says —
EN TÉ R A TE
DE
T US
DE RE CH OS.

Epilogue in the form of Footnotes

1. A Landay is a form of poetry formed in Afghanistan. Landay origins come from girls and women who were barred from reading and writing, so to pass on information, they would memorize these Landays and carry them to the next person's ears. They are rooted in themes of love and grief. I whisper these to a mother who loves me dearly and does not know how to love me (w)holy.

2. I love my mother dearly. I see her and see a woman made of survival and others' sorrows. She tells me that when I was in her womb, she no longer wanted to live. That people would tell her to stay with my father until he gets out. That the prisoner's wife has a duty to uphold until the sentence is done. "It will serve you well", they told her. So she did, with me in her belly. I am convinced I absorbed the battles yet to come of living a life I did not want to live to make sure my duty is upheld.

3. She is trying. In her own way, I think she is trying to be the mother I needed her to be.

4. I know what it is to be riddled with fear of losing someone you love so dearly to damnation; the church is good at that. I hold empathy for my mother while the child in me is also asking to be picked up - and between the two, most of the time, I choose my mother, as I always have.

5. The church taught how to be a good Martyr. Taught me to shed myself if needing a reason to live other than Jesus himself, I do not think they expected me to be a Martyr for love. A Martyr for children who suffer. A Martyr for those in my community who need a hand to hold while they pass on.

6. I love her so much. Everything reminds me of her. Mourning the living is a heartbreak I wish upon no one. With this grief, if we choose to talk to the dead, there's a good chance they will answer us back.

Rosa María Sandoval[6]

Standing at 5'1", all three of her children tower over her.
She's adopted many more, none of them officially,
but many in the church. Call her *Mami*
as if they were birthed from her womb
and she accepts it as if she thoughtfully chose
the names by which they introduce themselves.

She's fed entire cities, known for the magick
held between her palms. She sat with the sinners
before she knew that people could be sinners.
Always with a mound of pupusas y cortido placed
in front of them and plenty of styrofoam
containers for the road.

I haven't spent a birthday with her in nearly 10 years
but soon, she turns 60. She is the reason why
birthdays are so difficult. For as long as I can remember
I was met with large bouquets of flowers and a thousand balloons.
If no one else remembered, she would.
If there was a party of 100 people, she planned it.

She loves to garden, and every room in her
home is adorned with a hammock. She cries often
from self-induced laughter. Holding up a carrot, unable to contain
herself as she sets up the joke of how large the harvest was
this year just to be met with the tiniest one of the bunch.
Quietly - she finds beauty in everything.

She is missing one of her teeth, making her smile
that much more memorable. She believes the lessons
that she's taught us are so forgone by assimilation
and I don't know how else to remind her that she lives in my bones.
I wake up with an intense craving for neugados one morning
and weave my way through grocery aisles for yucca y miel.

---

[6]   I love her so much. Everything reminds me of her. Mourning the living is a heartbreak I wish upon no one. With this grief, if we choose to talk to the dead, there's a good chance they will answer us back.

And I can't even remember the last time I had any.
I call my mother for her recipe, every time
with a sweet delight in her voice that her child is carrying
traditions in their own way. And I do everything
for her delight in me. To show her in so many ways
I cannot escape wanting to make her proud of me.

It's why I left.

Rosa María Sandoval

De pie, con una altura de 5'1, sus tres hijos
la dominan. Ha adoptado muchos más, ninguno
de ellos oficialmente, pero muchos en la iglesia.
La lamallan mami como si hubieran nacido de su
vientre y ella lo acepta como si hubiera elegido
el nombre con el que se presentan.

Ella ha alimentado a ciudades enteras, conocidas por su magia
sostenida entre sus palmas. Ella se sentó con los pecadores
antes de saber que las personas podían ser pecadoras.
Siempre con un montón de pupusas y cortido colocado
delante de ellos y mucha contenedores para la carretera.

No he pasado un cumpleaños con ella en casi 10
años pero pronto cumplirá 60. Ella es la razón por la que
los cumpleaños son tan difíciles. Desde que puedo recordar
me recibieron con grandes ramos de flores y un mil globos.
Si nadie más lo recordaba, ella lo haría.
Si había una fiesta de 100 personas, ella lo planificaba.

Le encanta el jardín y cada habitación de la casa
está adornada con una 'maca. Ella llora a menudo de
risa autoinducida. Sosteniendo una zanahoria, incapaz de contener
ella misma mientras prepara el chiste de cuán grande fue la cosecha
este año solo para encontrarme con el más pequeño del grupo.
En silencio, ella aencuentra la belleza en todo.

Le falta uno de sus dientes, lo que lo hace su sonrisa
tan memorable. Ella cree que las lecciones
que nos han enseñado ella olvidados por la asimilación y
no sé de qué otra manera recordarle que ella vive en mis huesos.
Me despierto una mañana con un antojo intenso de neugados y
me abro paso por los pasillos del supermercado en busca de yuca y miel.

Y ni siquiera puedo recordar la última vez que los tuve.
Llamo a mi madre para su receta, cada vez con
un dulce deleite en la voz que lleva su hijo

tradiciones a su manera. Y hago de todo
por su deleite en mí. Para mostrarle de tantas maneras
no puedo evitar querer que esté orgullosa de mí.

Y por eso, me fui.

Acknowledgments:

This collection would not have existed if it were not for, first and foremost, the community that Desireé Dallagiacomo has worked fervently at building for as long as I've known her. Through her guidance, the encouragement of my peers, and the utter inspiration I've gained/continue to gain from them, I have become the writer I am today. To KC, Oisín, and Elizabeth - I cannot express my eternal thanks for the hands y'all have laid on this book. You made me a better writer through your edits and encapsulated my heart/the heart of the book on the cover. To Caeli, who was in the room when the name of my book found me and who held my hand through the process of finding the works that would live here. To Liv, Josh, and everyone at Game Over Books, your belief in my work means more than I could ever express. To my brother who has been a lighthouse through the difficult transitions with my family I have experienced, thank you Fredy. Thank you for believing in me; there has never been a moment where I felt like you weren't my biggest cheerleader. Thank you for taking up the role of a father figure at a time when we were both figuring out how to be kids. To my sister Chachi, who loves me so unconditionally, I am thankful for the reminder of deep, deep love every time you reach out to me. To my best friends, my forged family, you kept my head above water these past few years. I'm partly alive because of you.

To all those growing up 1st Gen and fighting the path that has been precisely carved out for us, I write these stories for you to know you are not alone. To know that you can live a life authentically and beautifully. It comes with its specific trials and tribulations, but hold onto the moments filled with joy, laughter, and love. Those are the ones that helped me through the storm many nights. To all of my trans siblings, I love you! I love you so fucking much! God, you make this journey one of excitement. One I look forward to living, day in and day out. To all of the spirits that guide me, thank you for your protection. To all my ancestors, I hope there are parts of my stories that tell yours.

Para mi mama, sé que esperabas una vida muy diferente para mí. Lamento que no sea la de tus sueños, pero es la vida de mis sueños. Me enseñaste a luchar por eso, con uñas y dientes. Y eso es exactamente lo que he estado haciendo. Luchando con uñas y dientes por la hermosa vida que tengo. Te lo agradezco. Espero que puedas ver lo mucho que te amo y lo mucho que significas para mí.

Siempre te amaré.

Nancy Frenesy Azcona is a Queer, Trans, Two-Spirit multi-disciplinary artist who has taken their lived experiences and chosen to face the world through the bravery of vulnerability.

Nancy self-published their first chapbook, Corazón De Seda, in 2021, which is a collection of poems spanning across the author's adolescence into young adulthood. Hija De tu Madre/Atrevida is their second collection of poems. They are published in two anthologies and have performed for events/ organizations such as the Pay It No Mind Showcase, Body of Art Showcase, Identity Portrait Short Film for the Connie Norman Foundation, and Lady Gaga's Born This Way Foundation Re.Mixer. Nancy is a two-time fellow at The Heart of It Writing Retreat. Currently residing in Berkeley, California, Nancy facilitates writing workshops alongside Queer Arts collective D.I.Y. Museum and releases monthly works on their Substack.